THE SAD SACK

by SERGEANT GEORGE BAKER

SIMON AND SCHUSTER, NEW YORK

ALL RIGHTS RESERVED
INCLUDING THE RIGHT OF REPRODUCTION
IN WHOLE OR IN PART IN ANY FORM
COPYRIGHT, 1944, GEORGE BAKER
PUBLISHED BY SIMON AND SCHUSTER, INC.
ROCKEFELLER CENTER, 1230 SIXTH AVENUE
NEW YORK 20, N. Y.

Seventh Printing

MANUFACTURED IN THE UNITED STATES OF AMERICA

INTRODUCTION

Sometime just before or just after the beginning of the war, when I was whiling away the early years of my youth in a public relations office at Fort Bragg and sweating out the eventual end of my military career, I happened to pick up a copy of the camp newspaper and thus make an early acquaintance with one of the great military figures of our time.

Picking up the paper in the first place was purely accidental. People just didn't do that in those days. Camp newspapers were at the awkward stage; they had lost the small-town flavor of the Old Army and the Camp Newspaper Service hadn't come along to brighten their pages with such GI features as Milton Caniff's *Male Call* and Sgt. Leonard Sansone's *The Wolf*. Camp papers were half-civilian waifs, printed and sold by local civilian newspapers, written and edited by public relations soldiers whose jobs existed from day to day.

Having served as editor of the Field Artillery Replacement Center's section of the Fort Bragg Post, I can remember well the dismal stuff we used to fill the gaping columns of that wistful weekly. At times I had to use my own column. The Motorized and Animal Area (Artillery) was in even worse shape; it frequently resorted to publishing in its section an extremely corny imitation of *Dere Mabel,* written by a sleepy mule-skinner named Joe McCarthy, who later became an honest man as managing editor of *Yank.* His present exalted position calls for very little writing except for occasional nasty letters to overseas *Yank* correspondents.

But things in those days were so bad that any time a public relations man or a civilian publisher came across something unusual that he didn't have to pay for, it went into his camp paper just like that. That's the way George Baker went in.

Some civilian organization ran a contest for soldier artists and George submitted one of his cartoons. Nobody remembers anything now about the contest or its winners, but the sponsors of the contest got a helluva lot of publicity. They sent out free art to all the camp papers and the only editors who didn't run Baker's cartoon were those who were just too damned tired to open their mail that day.

The cartoon in question was something new, although not altogether startling then, on the American military scene. There was no caption of sparkling wit beneath it, there was no weird or uproarious action in its situation. There was nothing there but the title—*Inspection,* I think it was—and twelve drawings of a sad and extremely droopy-looking draftee.

In the first drawing this pathetic dogface lay supine and sloppy upon his tousled bunk, oblivious to the filthiness and disorder that characterized his little corner of the barracks. In the course of the next ten drawings he rose and made his bed, cleared away the scattered clothing and newspapers and old candy wrappers, swept and mopped the floor, pressed his uniform, shined his brogans, polished his brass, bathed, shaved, dressed himself immaculately, and stood at the foot of his bunk, trim and erect in the midst of sparkling order and cleanliness, while the inspecting officers passed on their rounds. In the last picture the inspectors had gone and our hero again lay supine and sloppy upon his tousled bunk, surrounded by the same scattered clothing and newspapers and old candy wrappers. It was the full military cycle caught in a newspaper cartoon.

Besides which, it was funny as hell.

When the new Army magazine, *Yank,* began to collect a staff in May of 1942 a small number of the craftier public relations writers of Fort Bragg managed to edge their way in on the deal. The first sight I saw as I walked into *Yank*'s new editorial rooms was the desk of Douglas Borgstedt, *Yank*'s original feature editor, who unloaded the job on Harry Sions, who in turn dumped the thing on me. Smack in the middle of the desk lay a large comic strip featuring our old friend, the sad and raunchy draftee. The title had been inked in as *The Sad Sack;* the strip had been selected as the first permanent feature of the new magazine.

I think it was a symbol of the death of the old, deadening camp newspaper and of the renascence of Army journalism.

The Sad Sack's popularity began with his first appearance in *Yank* in May of 1942 and has grown swiftly and steadily ever since. His name and his familiar, sagging likeness have decorated the sides of planes and tanks on every battlefront. Fan clubs have been formed by groups of stripeless soldiers who like to sit around in the evening, drinking three-point-two and likening themselves to their questionable hero.

Any number of admirers have written to Baker demanding that the Sack be promoted to private first class. More than one soldier has sent a pair of single stripes to him and at least one private first class has offered to relinquish his own rank to the Sack.

This clamor for promotion of the Sack leaves Baker cold. "Why should *he* get a promotion?" he used to ask. "There are a lot of guys in the Army who deserve a raise more than he does. Look at *me*. I've been a buck sergeant myself for two years now!" This, I feel, is a morbid and inexcusable attitude and one which I am unable to understand, especially since George Baker is now a staff sergeant. I will have been a buck sergeant for two years come next January (and for three years the following January) but I cannot hold this against the Sad Sack. Personally, I should like to see both of us promoted.

This feeling of sympathy and brotherhood with the Sad Sack is predominant in the Army and helps to explain his fantastic popularity. Large numbers of his fans write in to say that they have been through the same difficulties as the Sack went through in last week's strip; others write to tell Baker of troubles they have had and ask him to show how the Sad Sack would fare under the same conditions.

The Sack is the perfect personification of the Army's little man, the hopeless underdog who has no stripes, no glory, no friends in the orderly room, no escape from the dread terrors of red tape and higher ranks.

Since he is the Army's little man, none of his troubles are ever of his own making. No matter what he does or leaves undone, trouble will come to him from outside forces. The only thing he can ever be sure of is the perversity of fate.

The Sad Sack has come to realize that by now. He has learned to bow in philosophic resignation to whatever comes, and to hope for a lighter load tomorrow. So has George Baker, so have I and so have most of the Sad Sack's followers, all of whom are Sad Sacks to some degree.

SGT. MARION HARGROVE

THE PHYSICAL

THE UNIFORM

SGT. GEORGE BAKER

DRILL

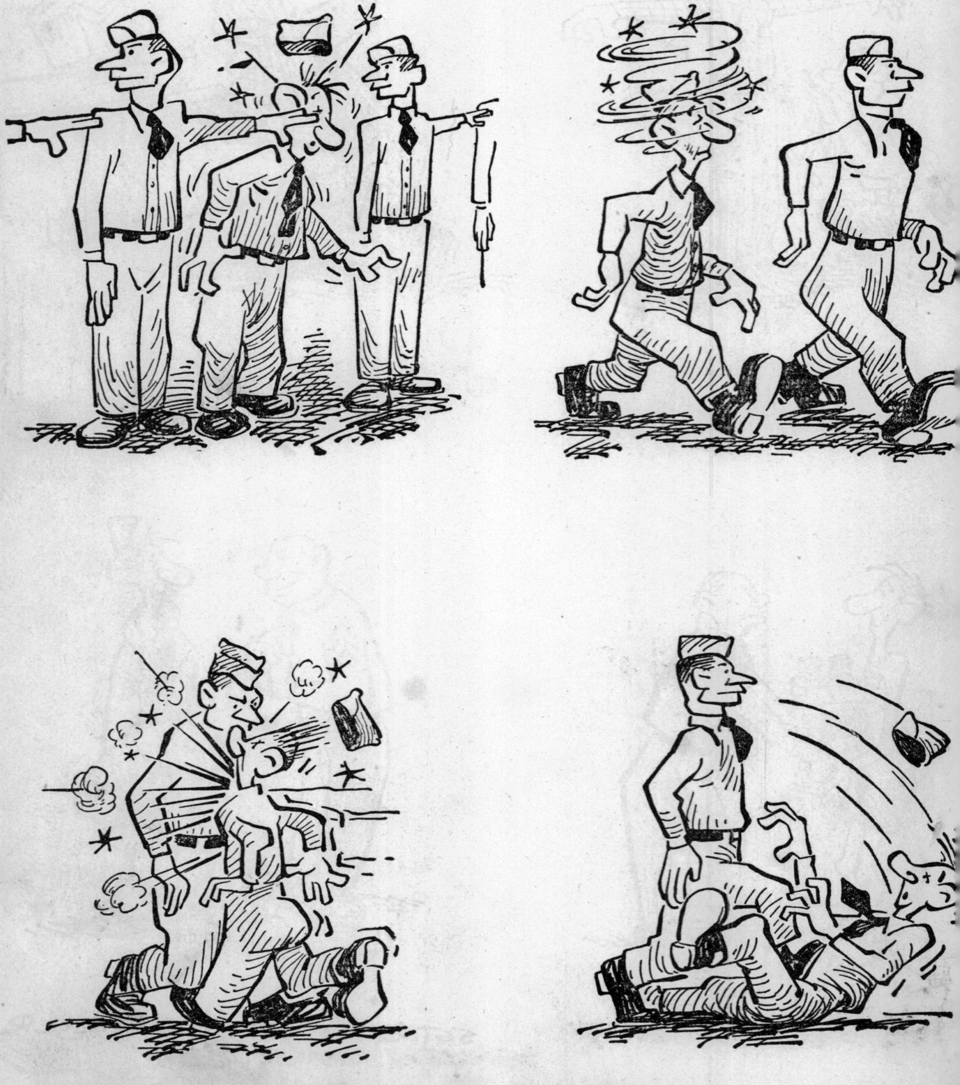

ORDERS

K. P.

PISTOL PRACTICE

SGT. GEORGE BAKER

INSPECTION

SICK CALL

SGT. GEORGE BAKER

THE PACKAGE

THE PACKAGE

SGT. GEORGE BAKER

PAY DAY

SGT. GEORGE BAKER

G. I. HAIRCUT

MORNING SHAVE

SGT. GEORGE BAKER

TABLE WAITER

SGT. GEORGE BAKER

THE MESSAGE

THE GOLDBRICK

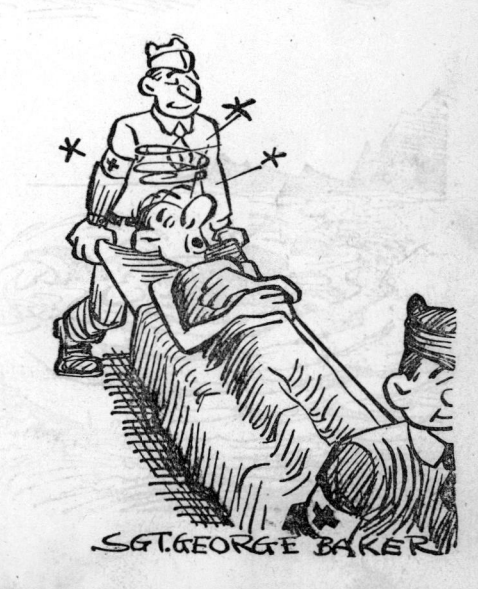

SGT. GEORGE BAKER

THE GOLDBRICK

SGT. GEORGE BAKER

IN TOWN

BOXING MATCH

SGT. GEORGE BAKER

BOXING MATCH

SGT. GEORGE BAKER

BUS STATION

SGT GEORGE BAKER

THE MARINE

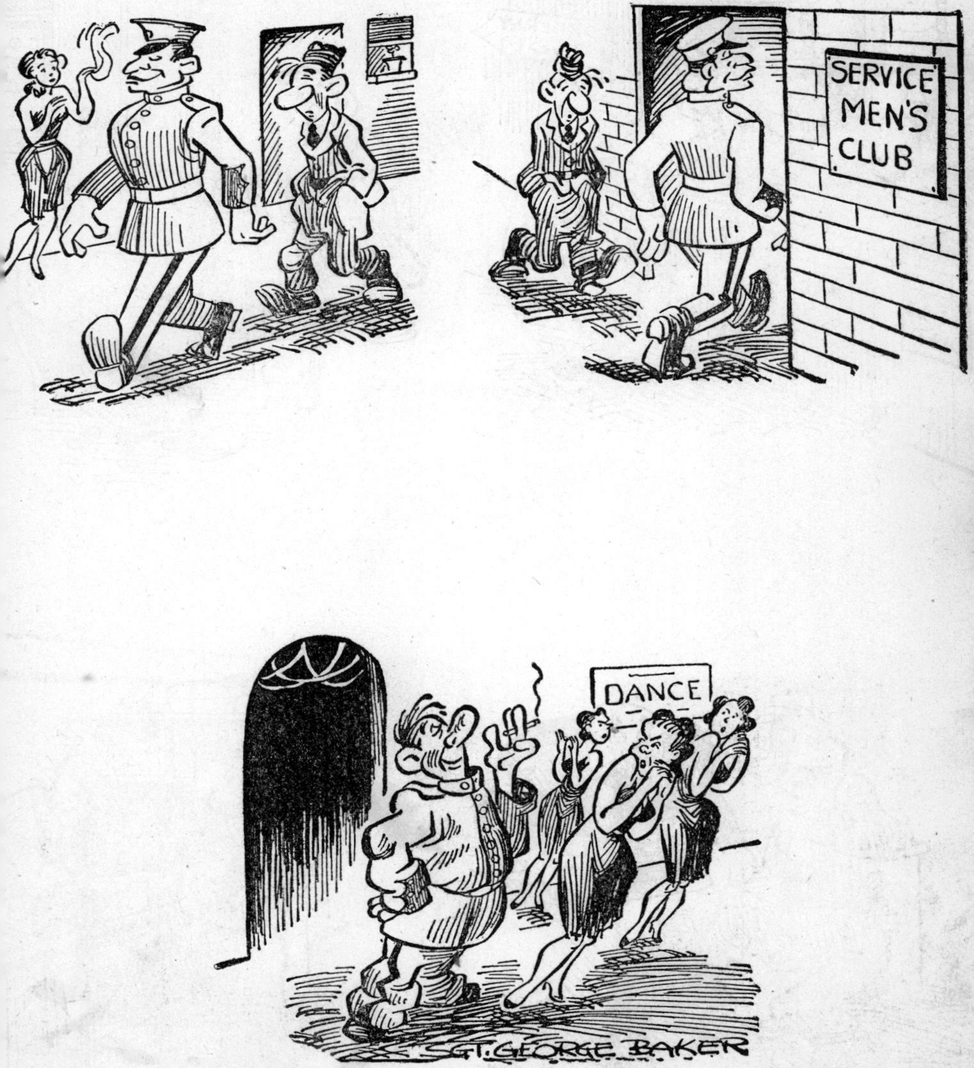
SERVICE MEN'S CLUB
DANCE
SGT. GEORGE BAKER

THE SHOELACE

SGT. GEORGE BAKER

SHOTS

SGT. GEORGE BAKER

THE MECHANIC

SGT. GEORGE BAKER

STRIPES

COMPANY COMMANDER

SGT GEORGE BAKER

THE TOPKICK

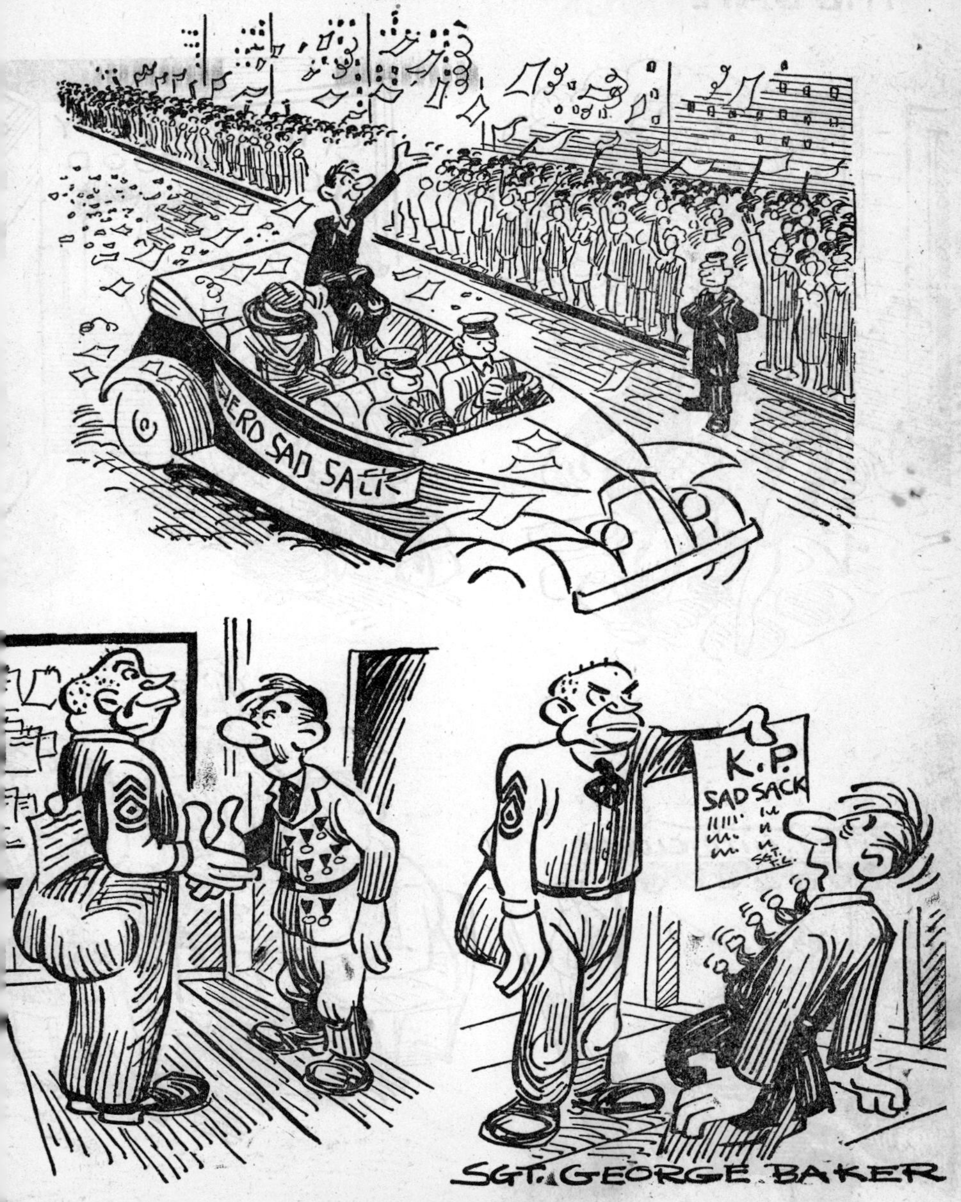
HERO SAD SACK
K.P.
SAD SACK
SGT. GEORGE BAKER

THE DATE

SGT. GEORGE BAKER

THE BULLETIN BOARD

MILITARY BEARING

MILITARY BEARING

LATRINE ORDERLY

SGT. GEORGE BAKER

LATRINE ORDERLY

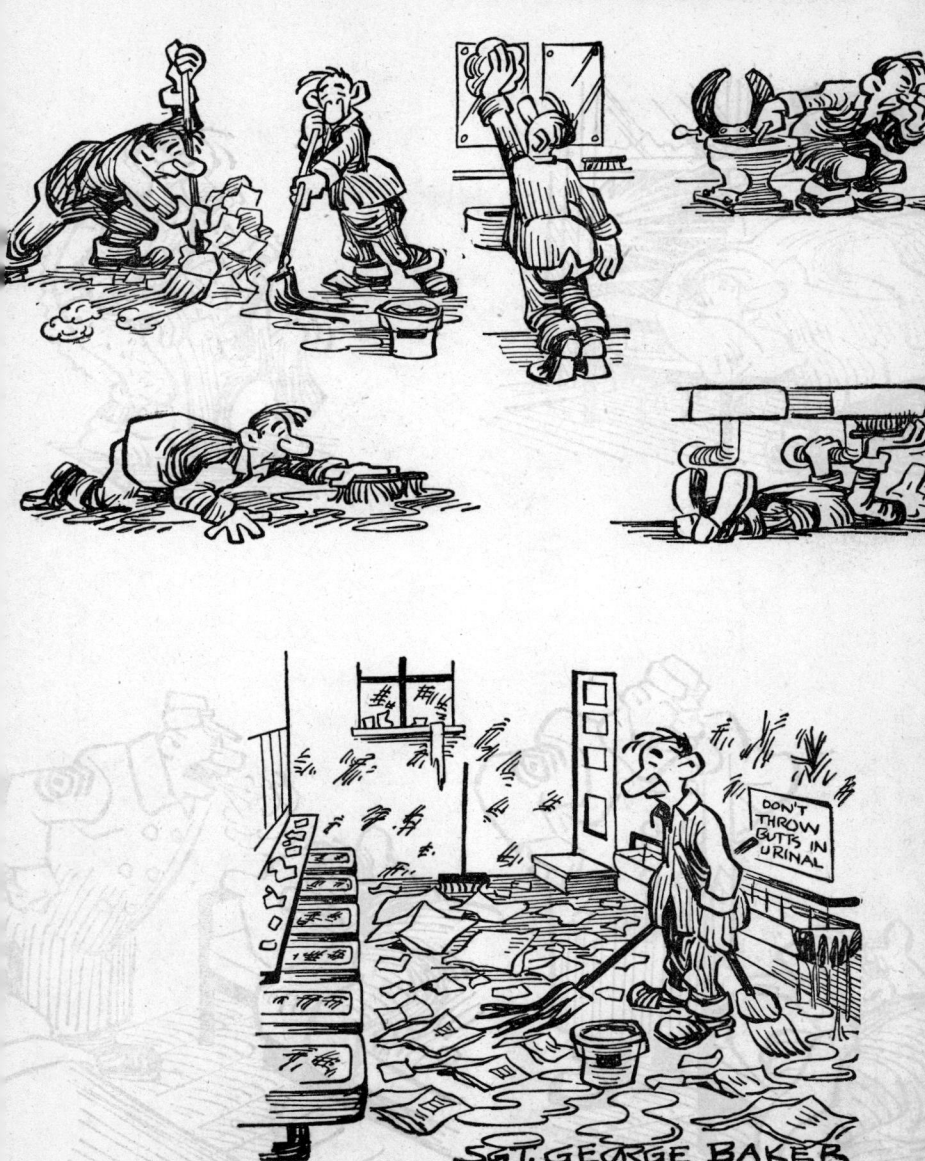

COLD MORNING

Sgt. GEORGE BAKER

COLD MORNING

BOREDOM

SGT. GEORGE BAKER

BOREDOM

THE CINCH

SGT. GEORGE BAKER

THE CINCH

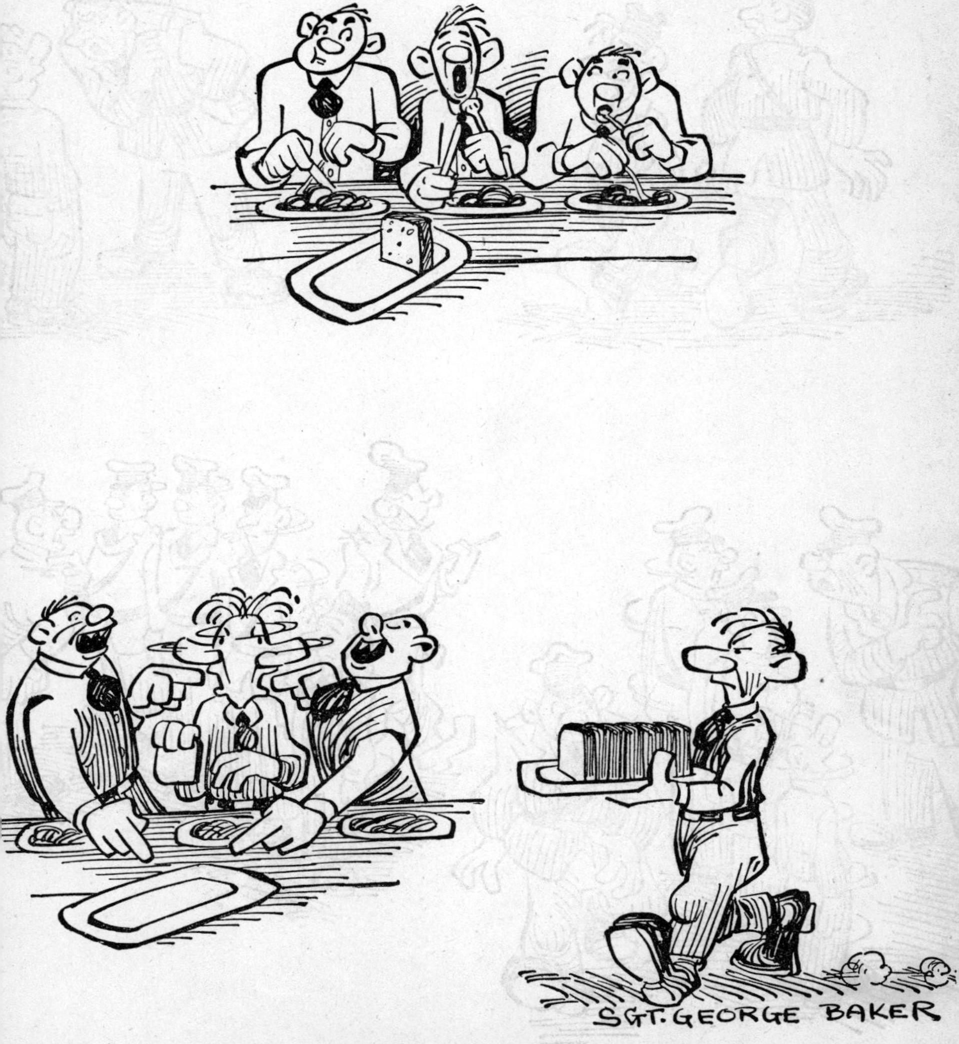

SGT. GEORGE BAKER

RANK

SGT. GEORGE BAKER

THE BAYONET

THE GOOD SOLDIER

SGT. GEORGE BAKER

THE GOOD SOLDIER

SGT. GEORGE BAKER

FIRST AID

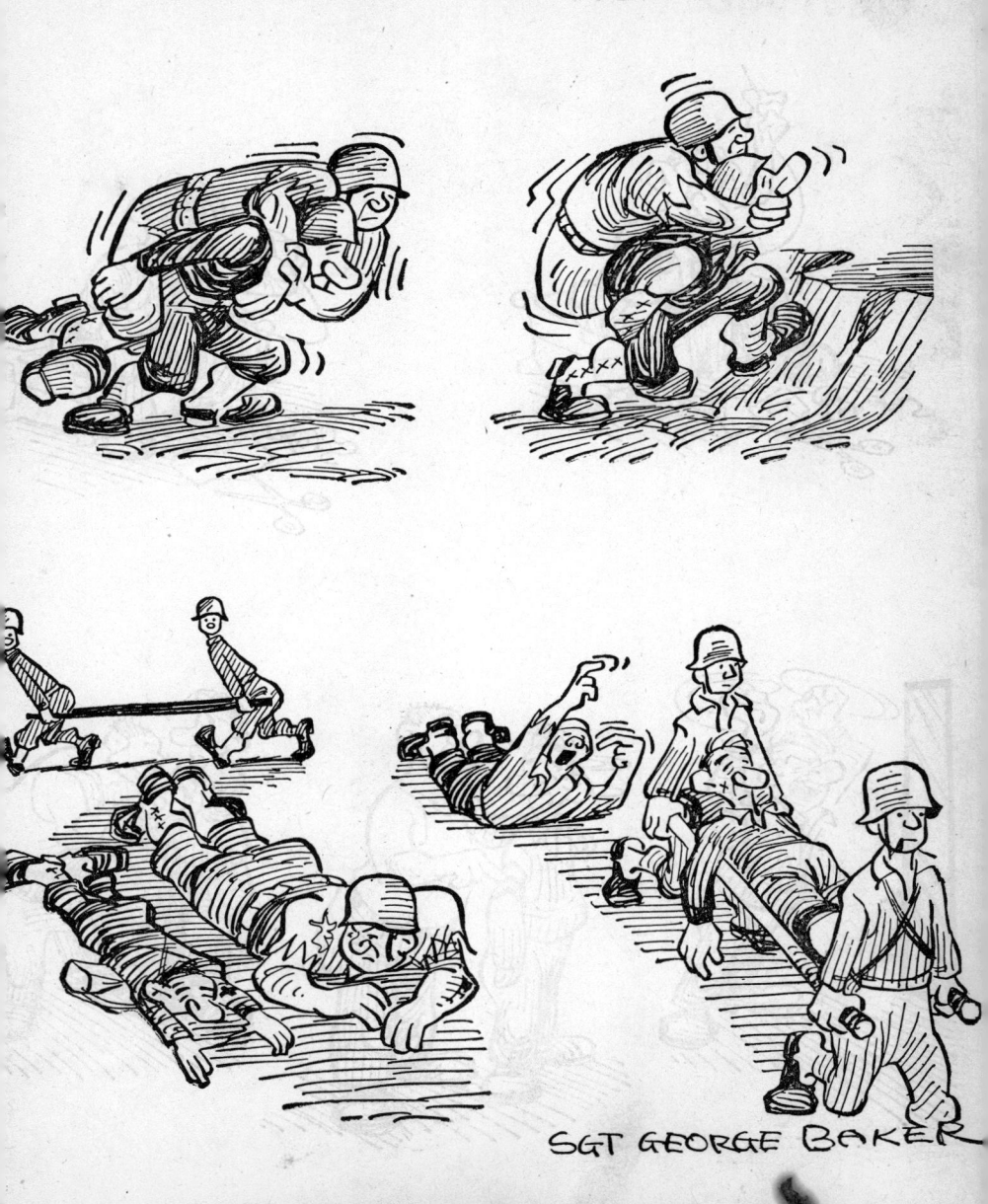

PROMOTION

SGT GEORGE BAKER

PROMOTION

SEX HYGIENE

SGT. GEORGE BAKER

SEX HYGIENE

SGT. GEORGE BAKER

SALVAGE

GOING TO THE P.X.?

SGT. GEORGE BAKER

GOING TO THE P. X.?

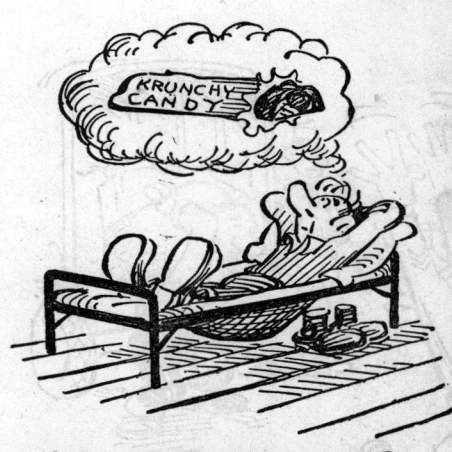

SGT. GEORGE BAKER

DOUBLE DUTY

CLOTHES EXCHANGE

SGT. GEORGE BAKER

CLOTHES EXCHANGE

SGT. GEORGE BAKER.

DUTY ROSTER

SYMPATHY

SGT. GEORGE BAKER

SYMPATHY

SGT. GEORGE BAKER

CHANNELS

THE OBSTACLE

SGT. GEORGE BAKER

THE OBSTACLE

SGT. GEORGE BAKER

VISITORS

SGT. GEORGE BAKER

THE M. P.

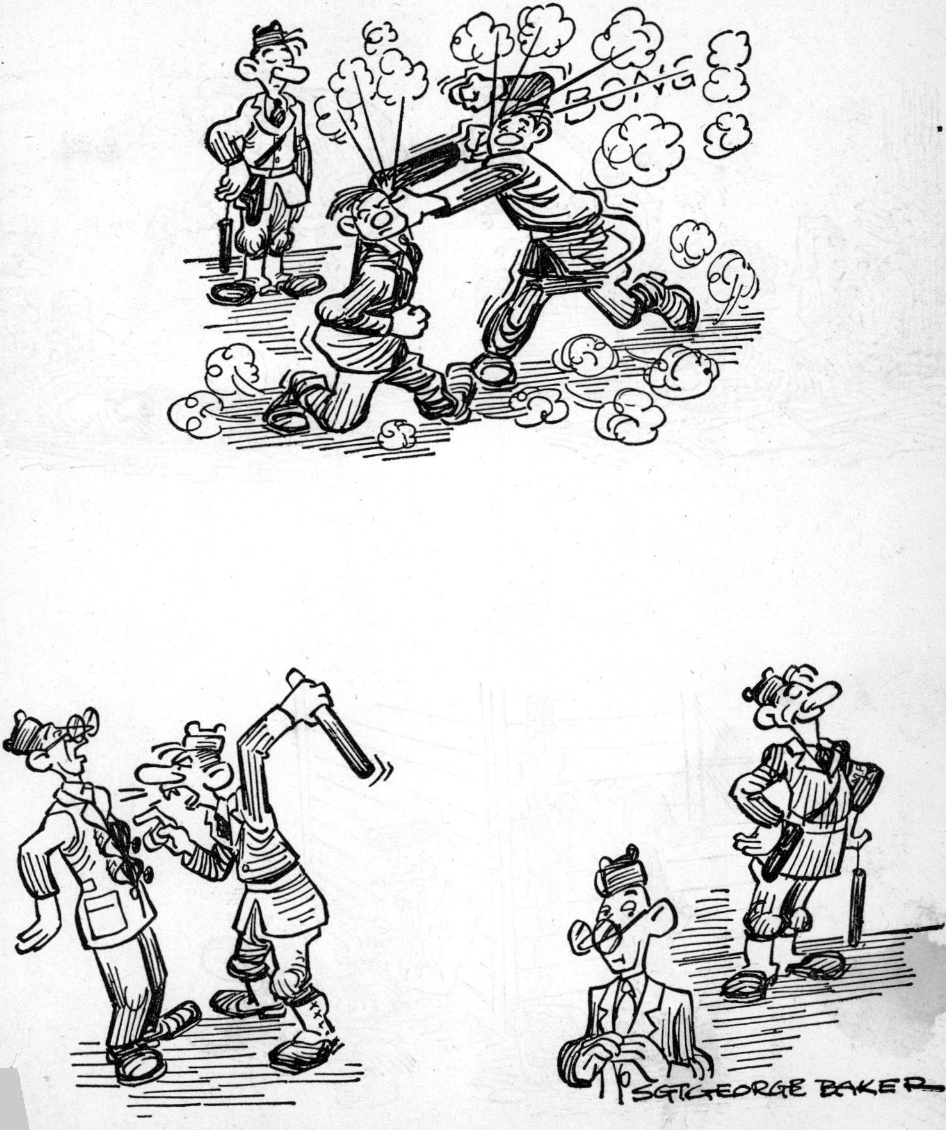
BONG
SGT. GEORGE BAKER

GOOD WORKER

WOUND STRIPE

SGT. GEORGE BAKER

WOUND STRIPE

SGT. GEORGE BAKER

BEER PARTY

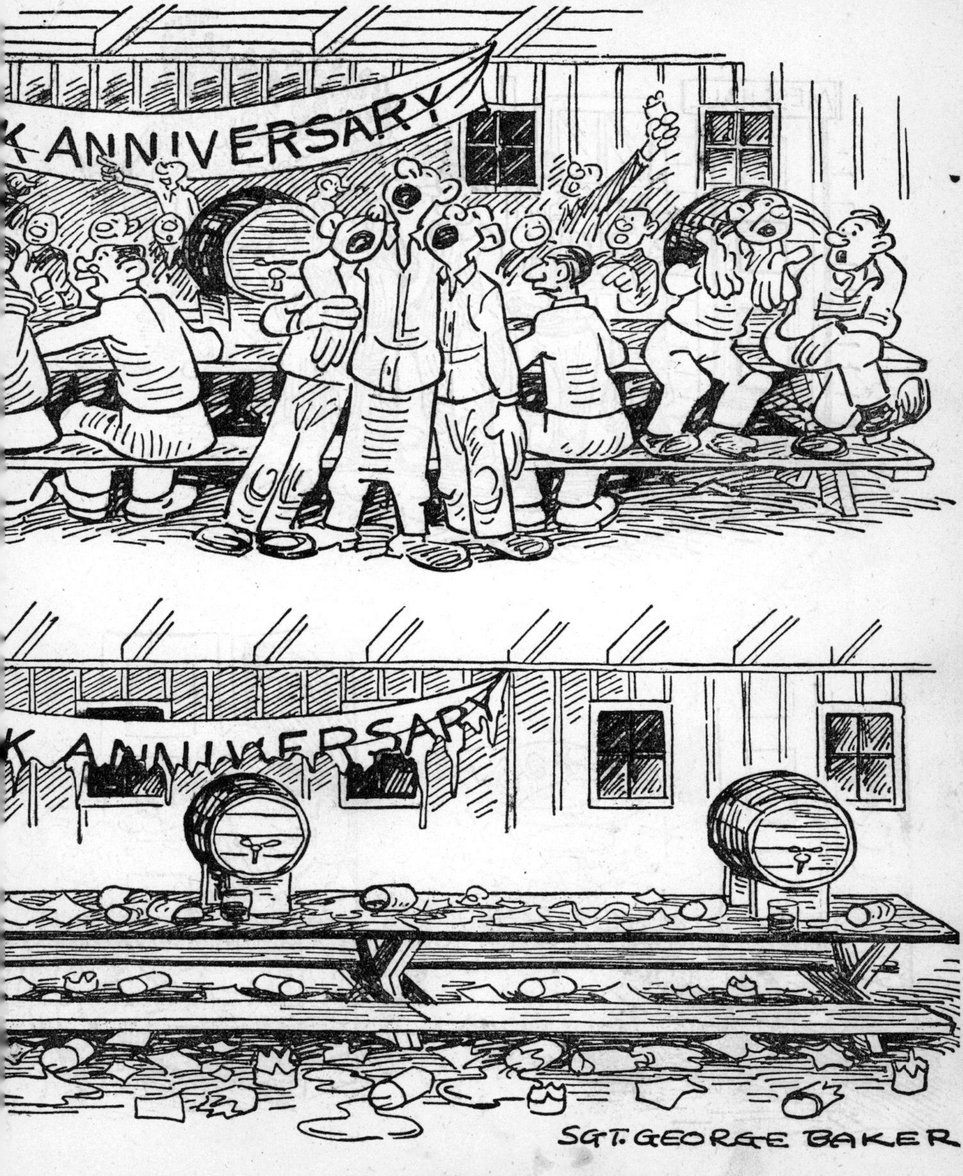
K ANNIVERSARY
K ANNIVERSARY
SGT. GEORGE BAKER

CHOW LINE

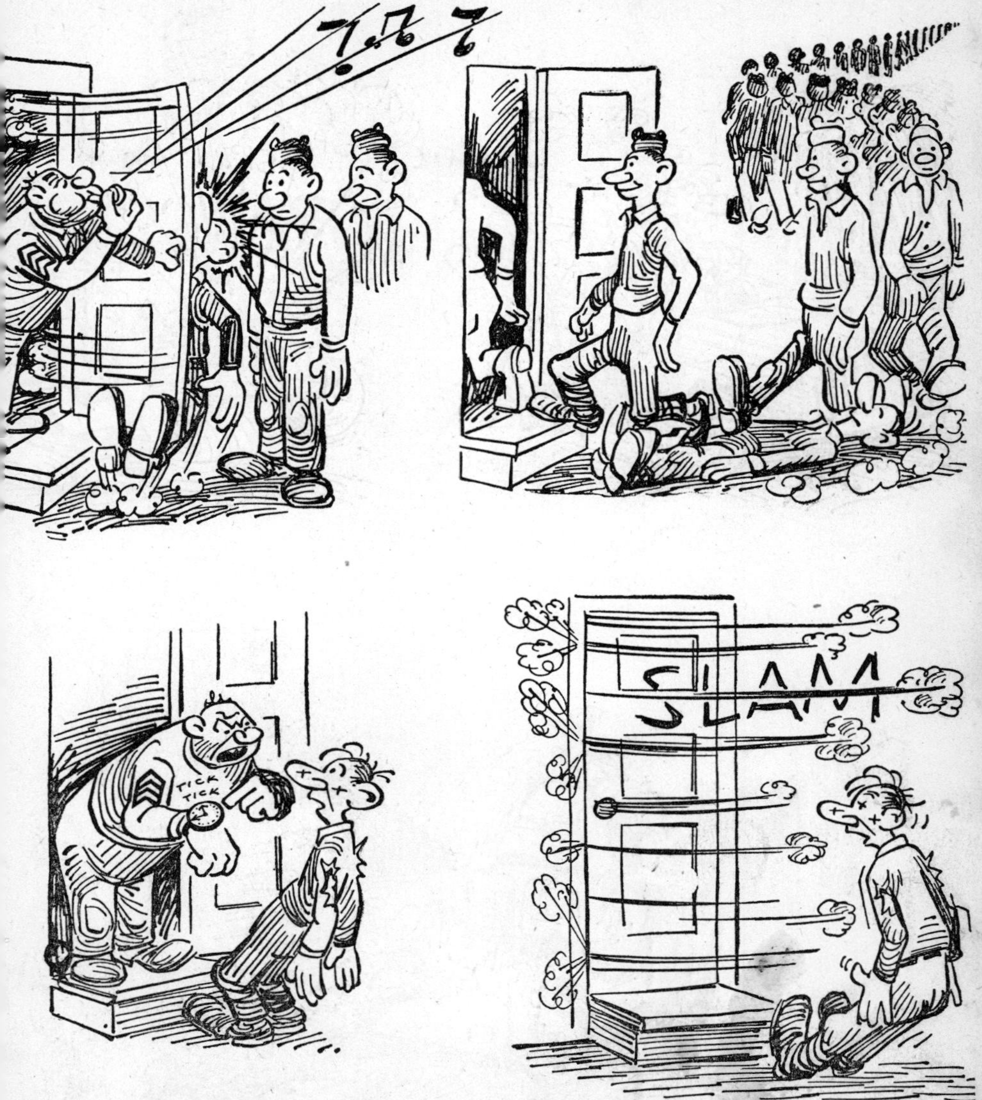
TICK
TICK
SLAM
SGT. GEORGE BAKER

THE CHAUFFEUR

PACKING

SGT. GEORGE BAKER

PACKING

Sgt. George Baker

SHORT RATION

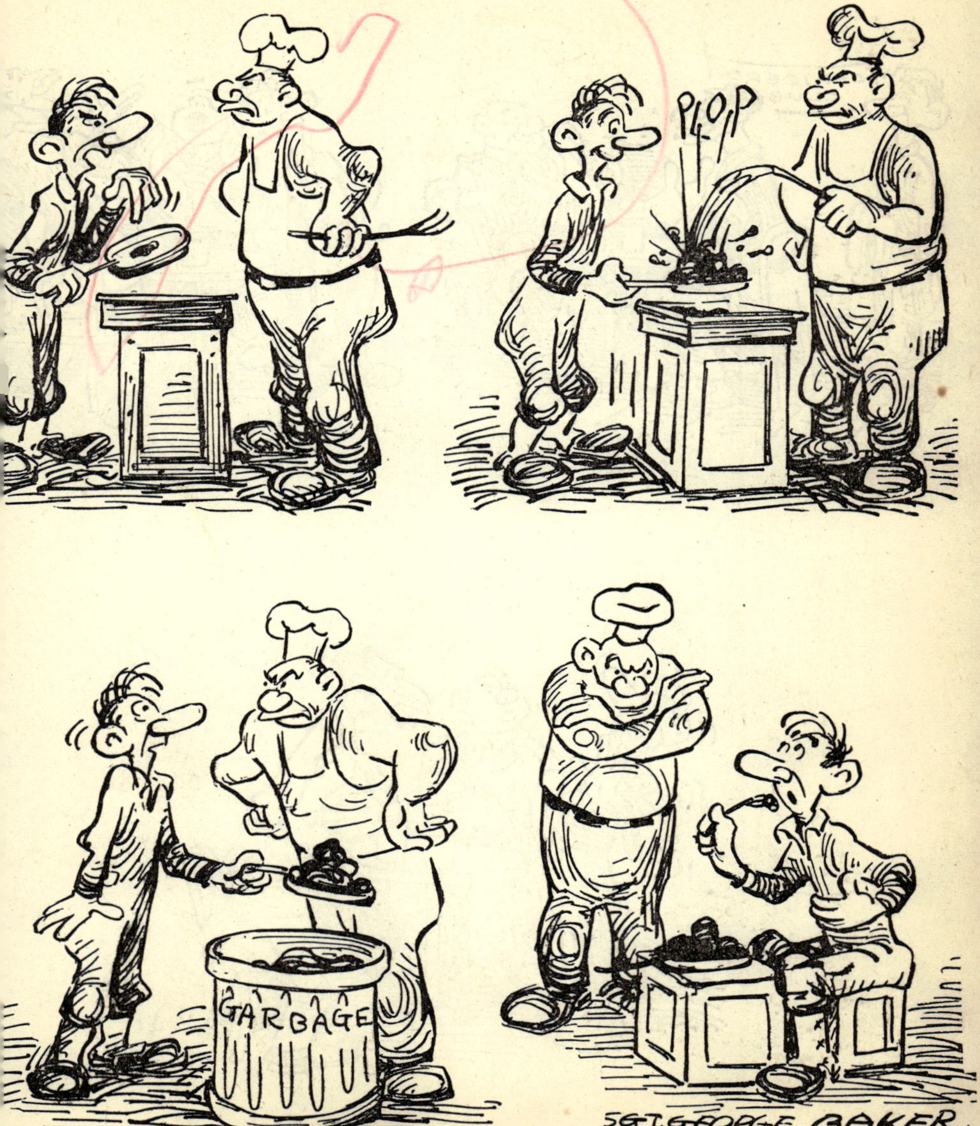
PLOP
GARBAGE
SGT. GEORGE BAKER

FUNNY STORY

SGT. GEORGE BAKER

SLIT TRENCH

SGT. GEORGE BAKER

TRANSFER

SGT. GEORGE BAKER

GARBAGE

SGT. GEORGE BAKER

THE NATIVE

SGT. GEORGE BAKER

OLD PAL

SGT. GEORGE BAKER

SNACK

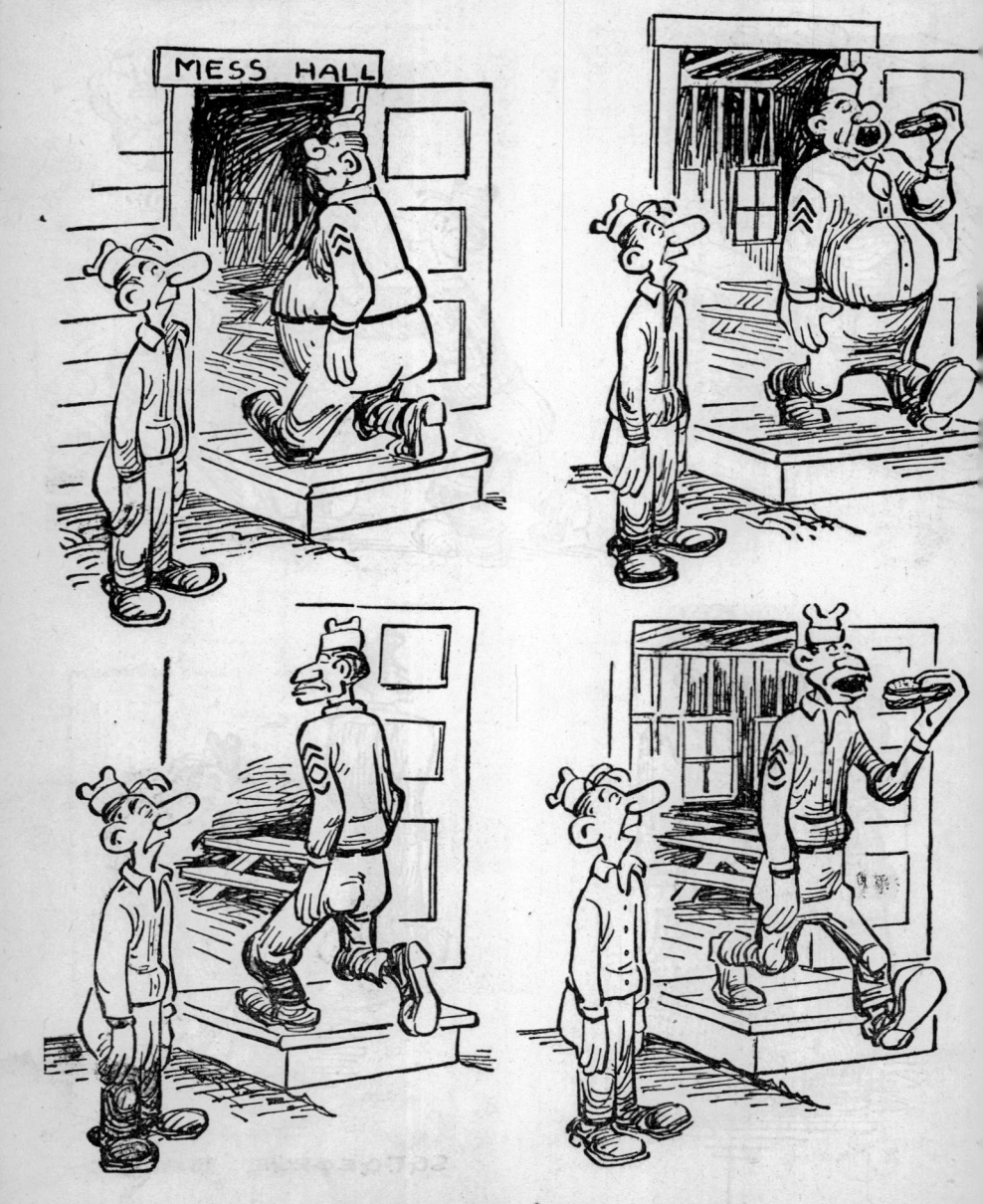

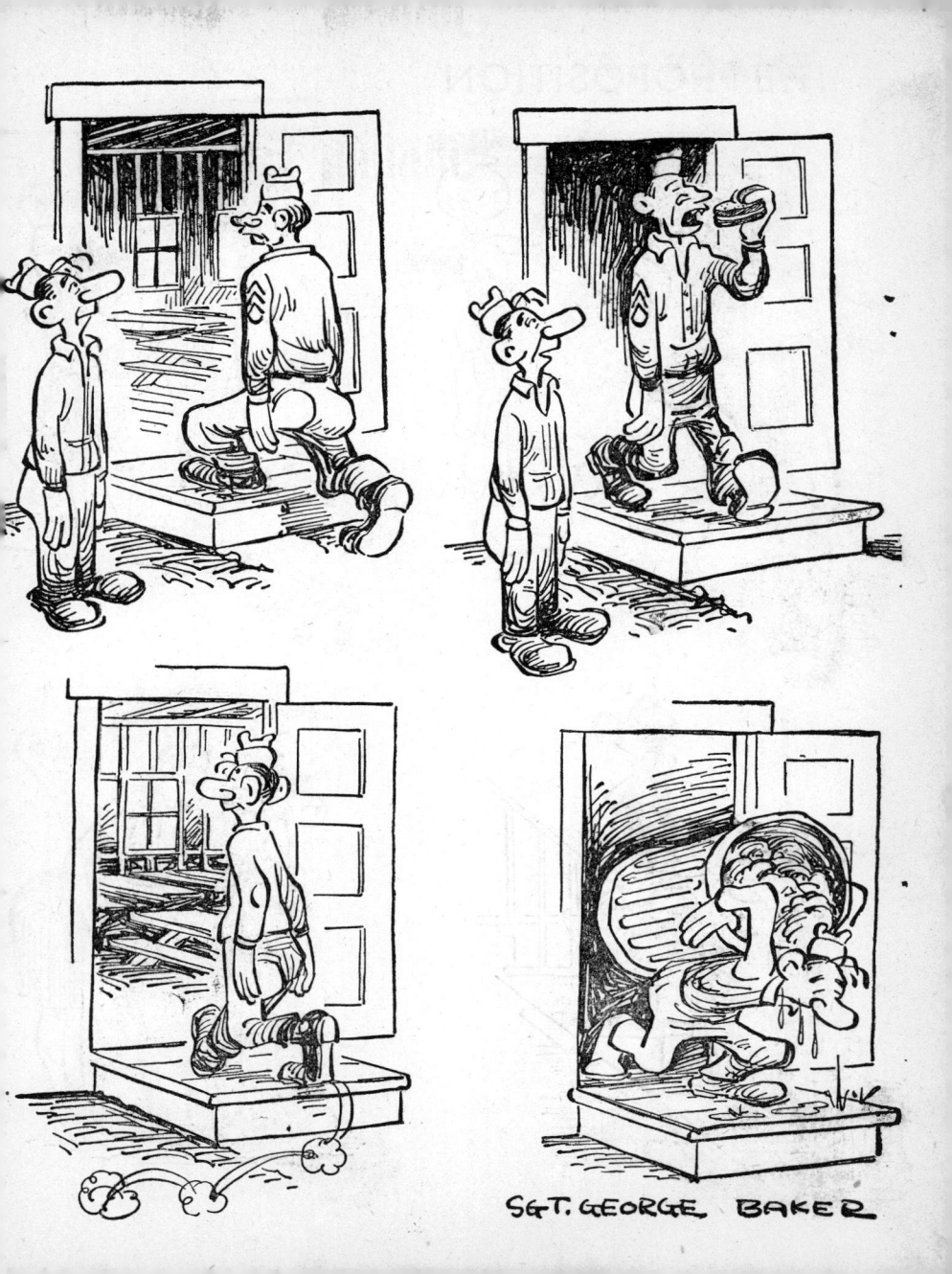

SGT. GEORGE BAKER

THE PROPOSITION

SHINE

SGT. GEORGE BAKER

SHINE

SGT. GEORGE BAKER

DOUBLE OUT

THE LEFTOVER

SGT. GEORGE BAKER

THE LEFTOVER

SGT. GEORGE BAKER

THE SHOWER

APPLE POLISHER

SGT. GEORGE BAKER

APPLE POLISHER

SGT. GEORGE BAKER

SLEEP

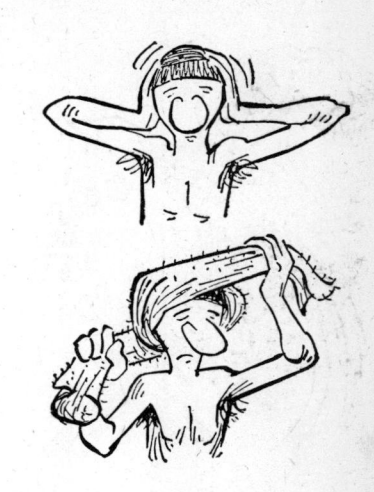

SGT. GEORGE BAKER

THE STRIPE

SGT. GEORGE BAKER

THE DEMONSTRATION

SGT. GEORGE BAKER

MAIL

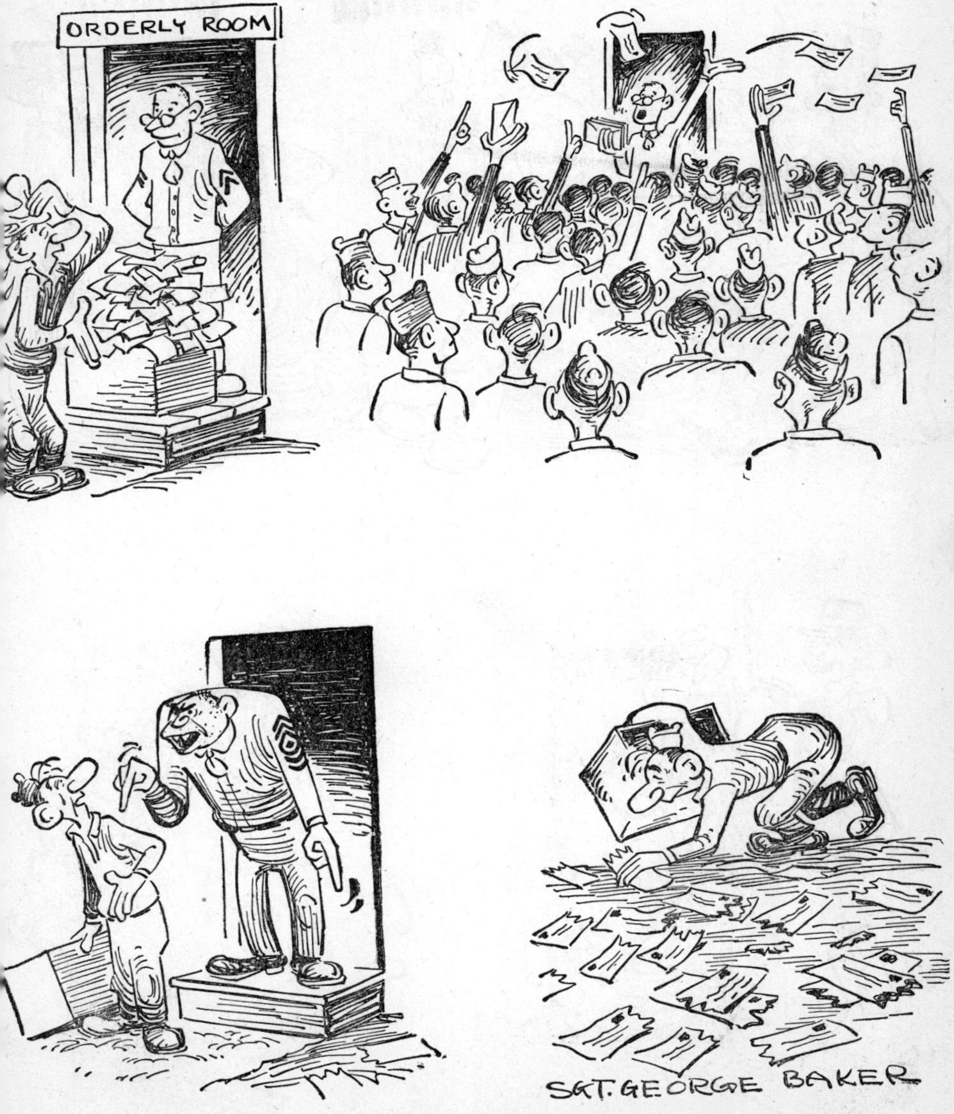
ORDERLY ROOM
SGT. GEORGE BAKER

EMBARKATION

SGT. GEORGE BAKER

ALLIED HARMONY

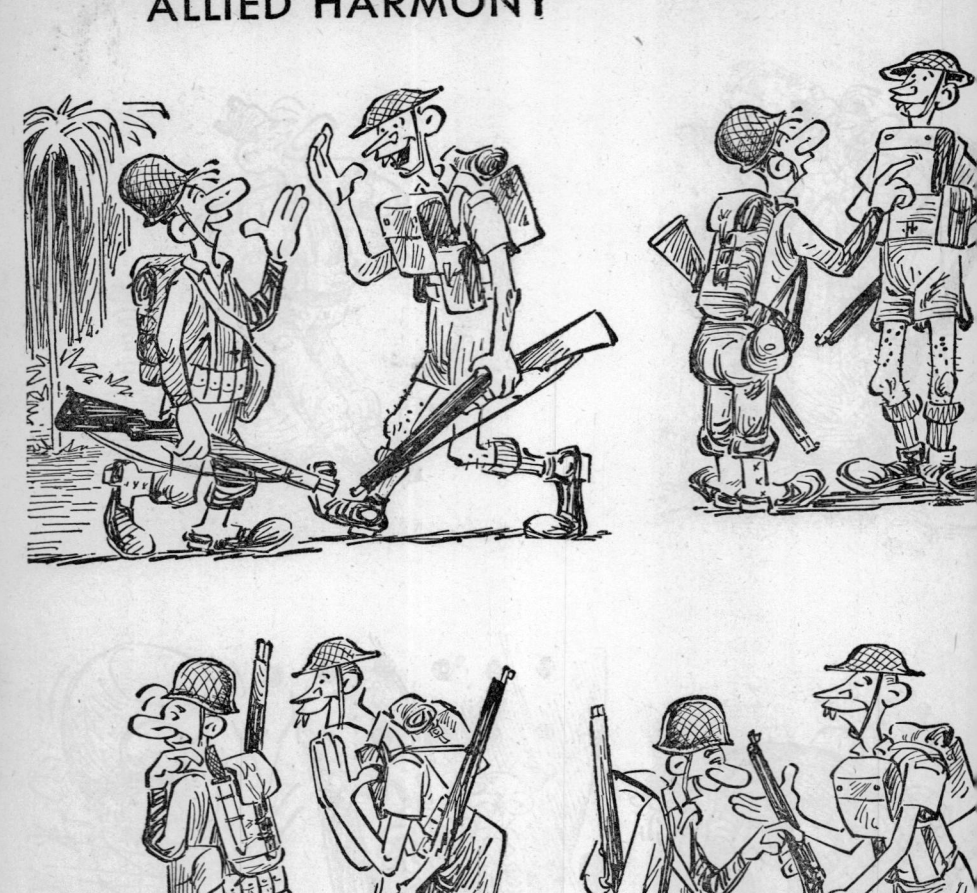

SGT. GEORGE BAKER

MORALE SHOW

SGT. GEORGE BAKER

LOST

SGT. GEORGE BAKER

OFFICERS ONLY

SGT. GEORGE BAKER

GOT A LIGHT, BUD?

SGT. GEORGE BAKER

GOOD DEED

SGT. GEORGE BAKER

MISSING CLOTHES

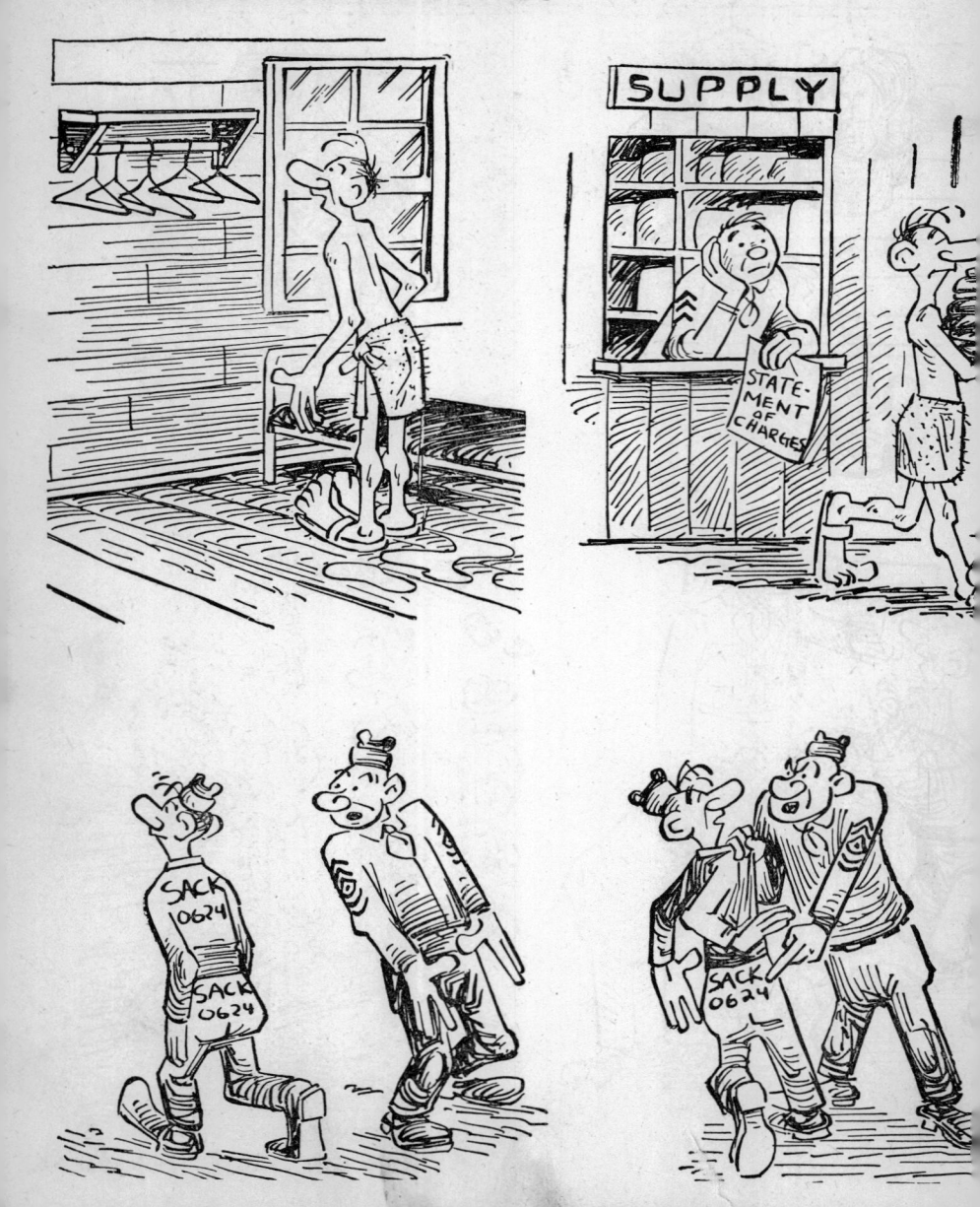

SGT. GEORGE BAKER

SHOVIN' OFF

SGT. GEORGE BAKER

STRATEGY

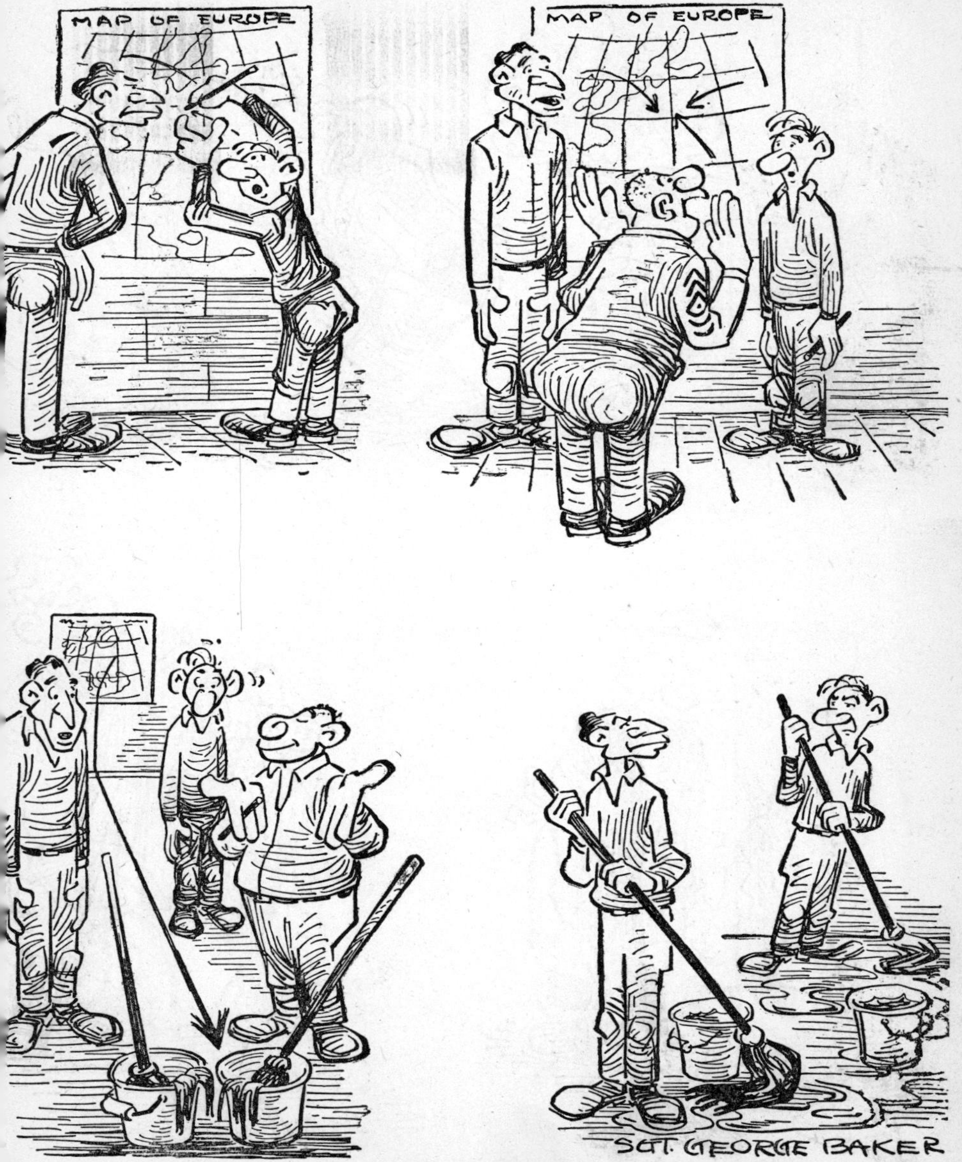
MAP OF EUROPE
MAP OF EUROPE
SGT. GEORGE BAKER

HUNGRY

SGT. GEORGE BAKER

ROUGH SEA

SGT. GEORGE BAKER

CHEAP LABOR

SGT. GEORGE BAKER

NEWS

SGT GEORGE BAKER

HABIT

SGT. GEORGE BAKER

V MAIL

SGT. GEORGE BAKER

FIRST COME—FIRST SERVED

SGT. GEORGE BAKER

SAFE SPOT

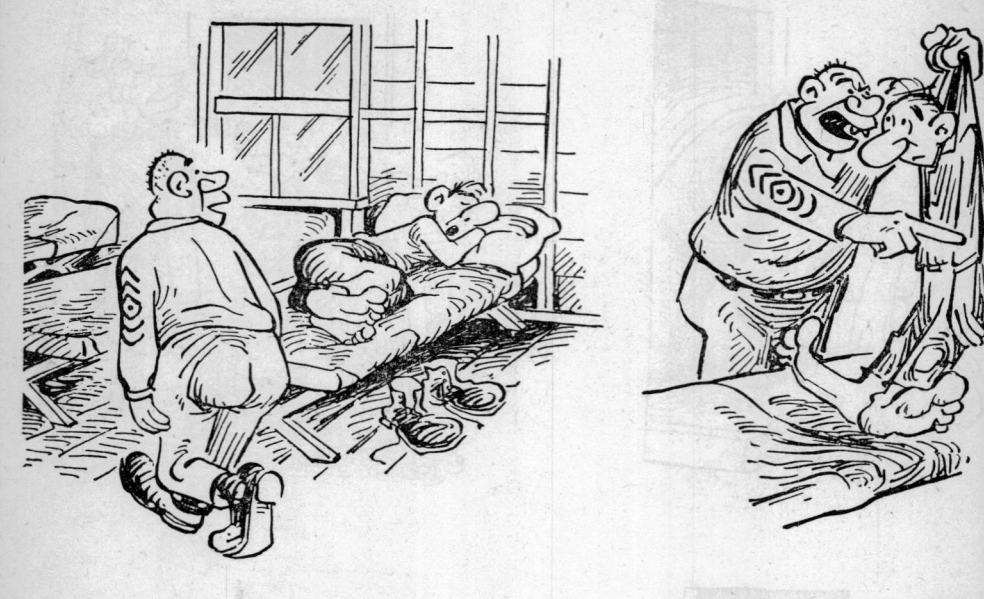

SGT. GEORGE BAKER

SOUVENIR HUNTER

SGT. GEORGE BAKER

TROPICS

SGT. GEORGE BAKER

EXCESS BAGGAGE

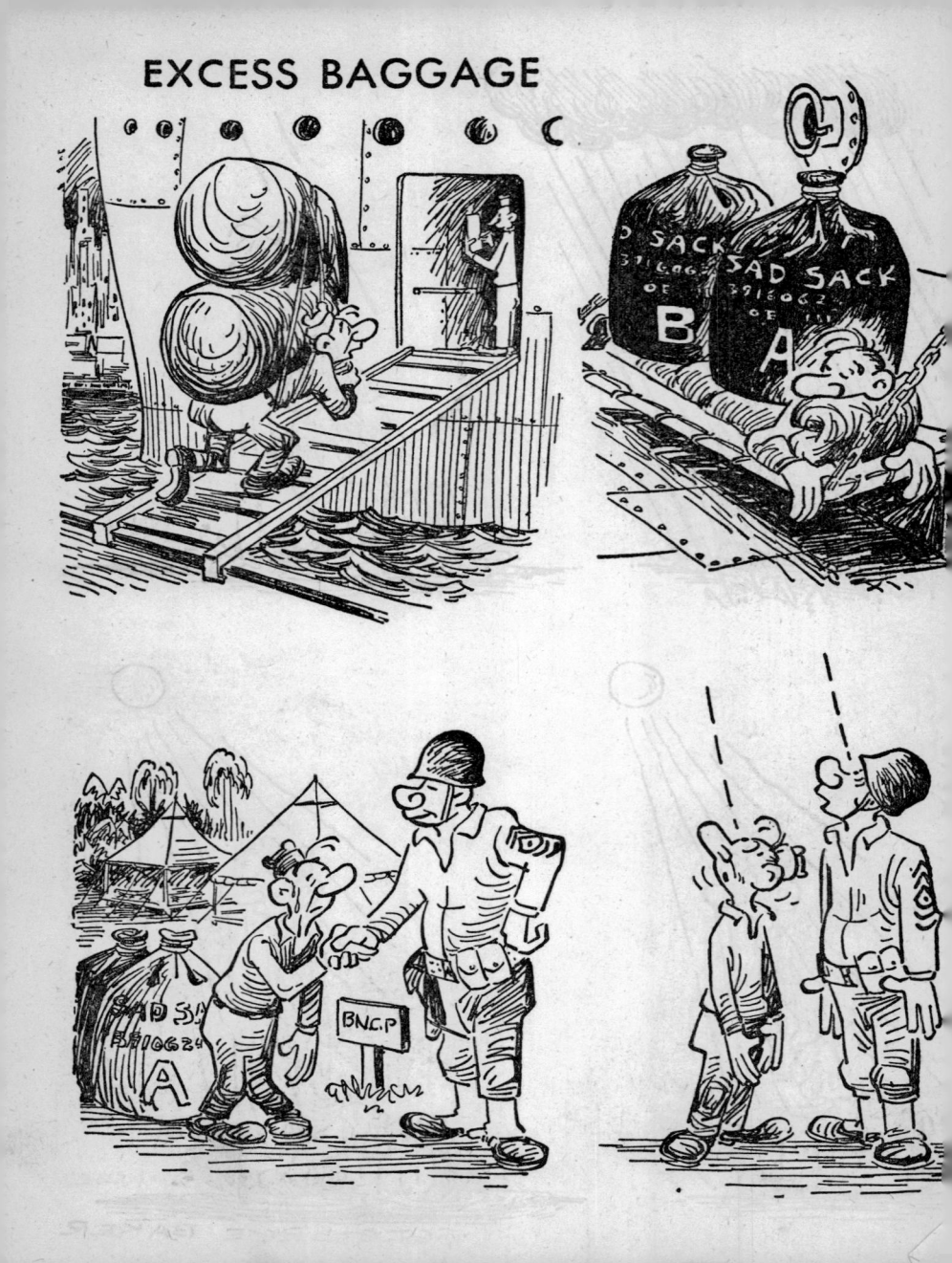

SGT. GEORGE BAKER

SPAM

SGT. GEORGE BAKER

GOOD NEIGHBORS

SGT GEORGE BAKER

REWARD

SGT. GEORGE BAKER

CLEANED UP

SGT. GEORGE BAKER

SUCKER

SGT. GEORGE BAKER

FINE SIGN

STOP!!
READ REGULATIONS BELOW
1- 25 MI. SPEED LIMIT
2- NO PASSING IN CONVOY
3- 50 YD INTERVAL
4- WINDSHIELD COVERED
5- COVERS OFF GUNS
6- OBEY MP DIRECTIONS
BLACKOUT REG.
SUPERIOR OFFS.
MP
TICKET
OBSERVE BLACKOUT REG
SUPERIOR OFFS.
VERLOADING VEH.
UN PREPARED
FIRING
LMETS ON
P.S. $25.00 FINE FOR STOPPING IN ROAD.
SGT. GEORGE BAKER

IMPRESSED

Sgt. GEORGE BAKER

EXERCISE

ENLISTED MAN'S RAG

SGT. GEORGE BAKER

ENLISTED MAN'S RAG

SGT. GEORGE BAKER

REAR GUARD

ALL WET

SGT. GEORGE BAKER

ALL WET

THE SPECIALIST

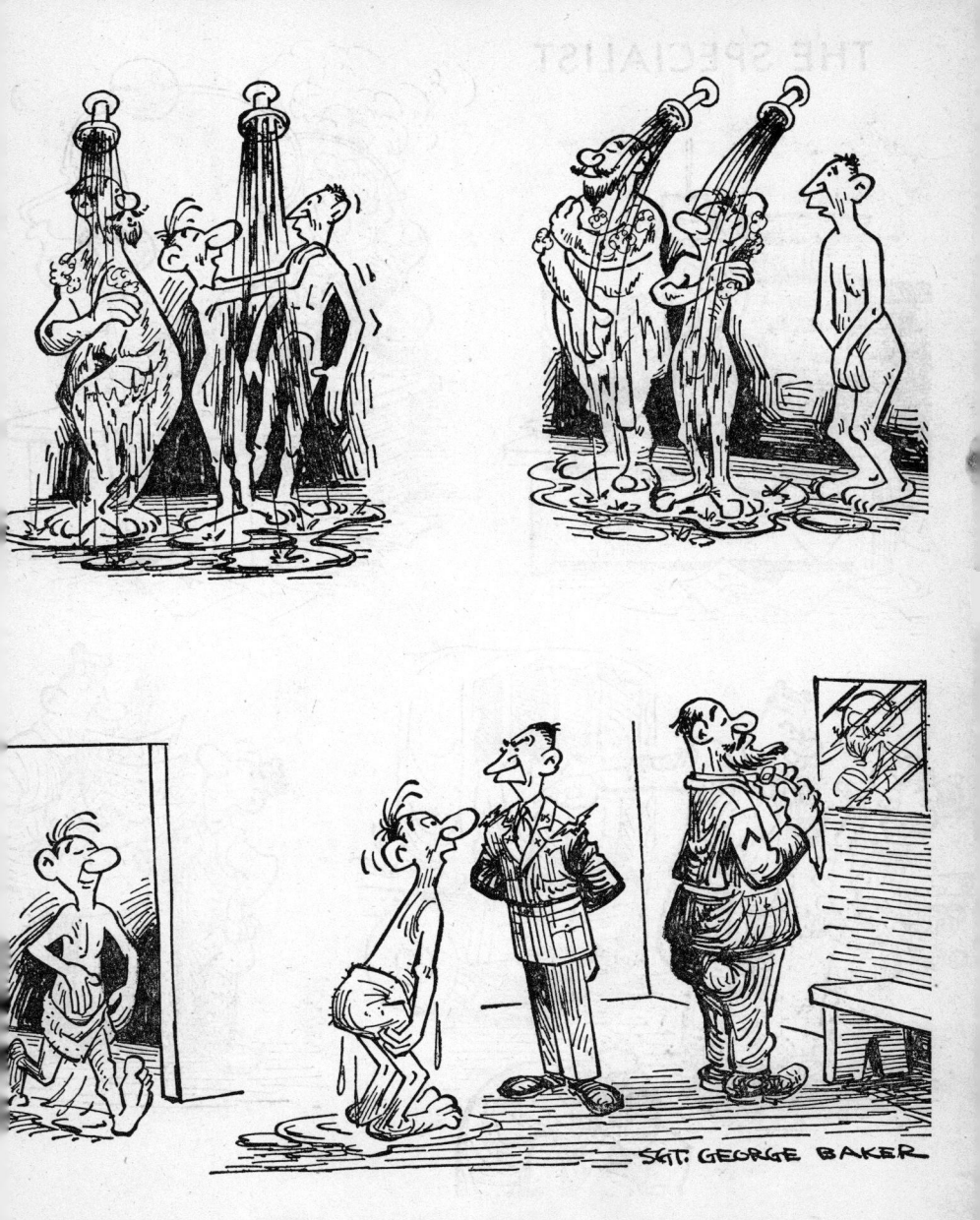

SGT. GEORGE BAKER

THE SPECIALIST

ARMY
SPECIALIST
SCHOOL
DIPLOMA
DIPLOMA
DIPLOMA
DIPLOMA
DIPLA
SGT. GEORGE BAKER

THE VICTOR

UNBURDENED

SGT. GEORGE BAKER

UNBURDENED

LOST AND FOUND

SGT. GEORGE BAKER

LOST AND FOUND

SGT. GEORGE BAKER

REST

SGT. GEORGE BAKER

INFORMATION

..DEPLORABLE CONDITIONS

SGT. GEORGE BAKER

DEPLORABLE CONDITIONS

REASSIGNMENT

SGT. GEORGE BAKER

REASSIGNMENT

EPORT BACK TO
THE U.S.A. FOR
REASSIGNMENT
OP33
SGT. GEORGE BAKER

Sgt. Gregor Duncan
Anzio – APR. 26 – 1944

About the Author

Sergeant George Baker writes: "I was born May 22, 1915 in Lowell, Mass.

Upon being graduated from high school, I did various jobs such as fitting the paper bags on newly pressed clothes in a cleaning and dyeing establishment, loading and driving trucks, and finally, working as an artist in a commercial art house. My artistic talents there were primarily employed in the drawing of pots and pans for newspaper advertisements.

In 1937 I went out to Hollywood to work for Walt Disney. For the next four years I worked on virtually all of his well known pictures which included Pinocchio, Fantasia, Dumbo and Bambi. From there I was inducted into the army in June of 1941.

Most of my evenings in the army were spent drawing cartoons of army life using the Sad Sack as the bewildered civilian trying to be a soldier. *Yank* magazine, which was then forming, invited me to join their staff.

To keep the Sad Sack abreast of developments, *Yank* has sent me to dozens of army camps, to Panama, Africa and Italy."

The drawing opposite was done by a very good friend, Sergeant Gregor Duncan, of the European *Stars and Stripes*, a short time before he was killed in the Allied advance on Rome.

About the Author

Sergeant George Baker where:II was born May 22, 1915 in Lowell, Mass.

Upon being graduated from high school, I did various jobs such as lifting the paper bags on newly pressed clothes in a cleaning and dyeing establishment, loading and driving trucks, and finally, working as an artist in a commercial art house. My artistic talents there were primarily employed in the drawing of pots and pans for newspaper advertisements. In 1937 I went out to Hollywood to work for Walt Disney. For the next four years I worked on virtually all of his well-known pictures which included Pinocchio, Fantasia, Dumbo and Bambi. From there I was inducted into the army in June of 1941.

Most of my evenings in the army were spent drawing cartoons of army life using the Sad Sack as the household civilian young-to-be a soldier. Yank magazine, which was then forming, invited me to join the staff.

To keep the Sad Sack abreast of developments, I not his sent up to dozens of army camps, to Panama, Africa and Italy.

The drawing opposite was done by a very good friend, Sergeant Gregor Duncan, of the European Stars and Stripes, a short time before he was killed in the Allied advance on Rome.

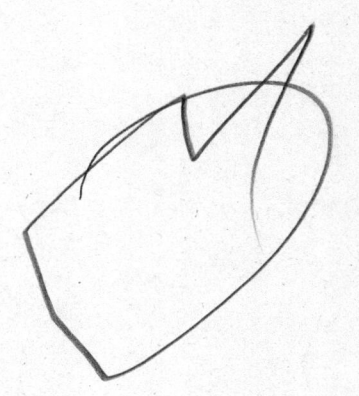

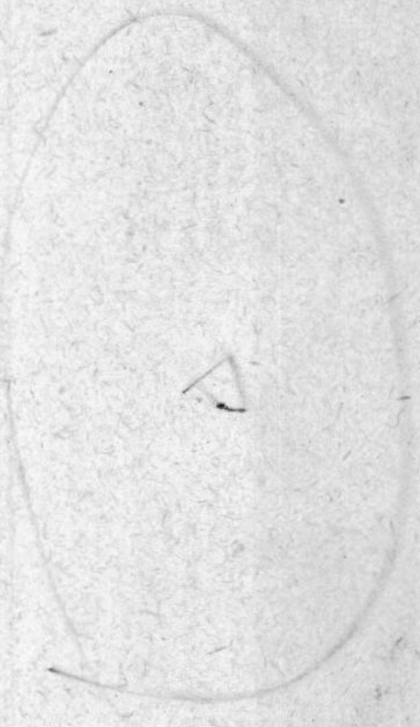